THE EFFECTS OF
CLIMATE CHANGE
ON THE OCEANS

By Natalie Hyde

CRABTREE
PUBLISHING COMPANY
WWW.CRABTREEBOOKS.COM

CRABTREE
PUBLISHING COMPANY
WWW.CRABTREEBOOKS.COM

Author: Natalie Hyde

Editorial director: Kathy Middleton

Editor: Janine Deschenes

Proofreader: Wendy Scavuzzo

Design: Margaret Salter

**Production coordinator
and Prepress technician:**
Margaret Salter

Print coordinator: Katherine Berti

Photo Credits:
b=Bottom, t=Top, tr=Top Right, tl=Top Left

Reef Quest Foundation: p11(tr), Dylan Vecchione

©Rolex/ Franck Gazzola: p13 (tr)

Shutterstock: Kobby Dagan, p14; ymphotos, p15 (tr); travelism, p18; IR Stone, p19 (b); MikeDotta, p26; Alexandros Michailidis, p27 (b);

Wikimedia Commons: Kolforn, p20; United Nations, Public Domain, p27 (t)

All other images from Shutterstock

Library and Archives Canada Cataloguing in Publication

Title: The effects of climate change on the oceans / Natalie Hyde.
Names: Hyde, Natalie, 1963- author.
Description: Series statement: Protecting the oceans |
  Includes bibliographical references and index.
Identifiers: Canadiana (print) 20200283774 |
  Canadiana (ebook) 20200283782 |
  ISBN 9780778782025 (hardcover) |
  ISBN 9780778782063 (softcover) |
  ISBN 9781427126061 (HTML)
Subjects: LCSH: Ocean—Juvenile literature. |
  LCSH: Climatic changes—Juvenile literature. |
  LCSH: Ocean-atmosphere interaction—Juvenile literature. |
  LCSH: Nature—Effect of human beings on—Juvenile literature.
Classification: LCC GC190.2 .H93 2020 | DDC j551.5/246—dc23

Library of Congress Cataloging-in-Publication Data

Names: Hyde, Natalie, 1963- author.
Title: The effects of climate change on the oceans / Natalie Hyde.
Description: New York : Crabtree Publishing Company, [2021] |
  Series: Protecting the oceans | Includes index.
Identifiers: LCCN 2020029744 (print) | LCCN 2020029745 (ebook) |
  ISBN 9780778782025 (hardcover) |
  ISBN 9780778782063 (paperback) |
  ISBN 9781427126061 (ebook)
Subjects: LCSH: Ocean--Juvenile literature. |
  Climatic changes--Juvenile literature. |
  Ocean-atmosphere interaction--Juvenile literature.
Classification: LCC GC21.5 .H93 2021 (print) |
  LCC GC21.5 (ebook) | DDC 551.5/246--dc23
LC record available at https://lccn.loc.gov/2020029744
LC ebook record available at https://lccn.loc.gov/2020029745

Crabtree Publishing Company
www.crabtreebooks.com   1-800-387-7650

Printed in the U.S.A./082020/CG20200710

Published in Canada
Crabtree Publishing
616 Welland Ave.
St. Catharines, Ontario
L2M 5V6

Published in the United States
Crabtree Publishing
347 Fifth Ave
Suite 1402-145
New York, NY 10016

Published in the United Kingdom
Crabtree Publishing
Maritime House
Basin Road North, Hove
BN41 1WR

Published in Australia
Crabtree Publishing
3 Charles Street
Coburg North
VIC, 3058

CONTENTS

REEF AT RISK

The Great Barrier Reef is the largest coral reef on the planet. It is made up of 3,000 individual reef systems and **coral cays**. The reef is home to an incredible amount of diverse sea life. Creatures such as humpback whales, clownfish, sea turtles, sea snakes, and giant clams live or feed around the reef. The reef's health affects the health of all the marine life around it. But climate change is putting the reef at risk.

Climate change is the change in our weather patterns due to higher levels of carbon dioxide in our atmosphere. Global temperatures are rising on the land and in the ocean. Since 1890, oceans have warmed up about ½ a degree Fahrenheit (0.2° C). This may seem like a tiny increase, but corals do not thrive in warmer seas. The Great Barrier Reef is dying.

Corals are living creatures that anchor together to build reefs. But as ocean temperatures rise, fewer new corals are building the reefs.

Changing Oceans

Other plants and animals in the oceans are feeling the effects of climate change, as well. Seagrass, for example, is home and food to many animals such as sea turtles. Seagrass meadows are dying off, leading to starvation in some turtles. Climate change is causing other problems, too. The levels of oxygen in our oceans are dropping. The water is also becoming more **acidic**. We need to take action to protect the valuable resources of our oceans.

Since 2016, half of the Great Barrier Reef has died.

CLIMATE CHANGE

Climate change is due in part to natural forces such as activity from the Sun or volcanoes. But much of it is also due to human activities. Through climate change, humans endanger ocean life. People are now aware of the effects climate change has on the oceans and are working to slow or reverse them.

We burn fossil fuels such as gasoline to move our cars, buses, trains, ships, and airplanes. We also use fossil fuels to heat our homes and for cooking. Burning fossil fuels releases carbon dioxide into the air. Farming and mining can release other gases such as methane and nitrous oxide. Like glass in a greenhouse, these gases act like a shield that does not let heat near Earth escape into space. Greenhouse gases cause our atmosphere to heat up, which causes our oceans to heat up.

93.4%
Into the oceans

With each increase in ocean temperature, more marine creatures are affected.

Widespread Impact

Our oceans are a vast body of water. They are so large that they have a constant temperature. In fact, oceans **moderate** temperatures on land. Land plants and animals are used to changing temperatures through the seasons. But marine plants and animals thrive in a habitat with the same temperature all the time. They become stressed or ill if the temperature changes. Every marine plant or animal that struggles or dies affects an entire food chain, including our food supply. Although this is a **critical** problem, many people are working hard to do their part to stop climate change and to lessen the impact it is having on the oceans.

DANGER TO DIVERSITY

Warmer ocean water temperatures cause many problems for marine plants, fish, sea birds, and mammals. Changing water temperatures force wildlife to migrate to new areas where they face threats to survival. Plants and animals that do not migrate must try to survive in warmer waters.

Fish and marine mammals are forced to move to new locations to find cooler temperatures. That can mean they migrate farther north, south, or into deeper water. These new areas may have more predators or not enough food.

Rising temperatures cause even more problems for plants and animals that do not move. They cannot seek out a more suitable area. Seagrass, kelp forests, corals, and sponges are all anchored to one spot. If the water temperature is too warm, they become stressed and even die. Corals react strongly to changing temperatures. When the water warms, they become stressed. They **expel** the bacteria living inside their structures that provide their food. Without the bacteria, they turn from a healthy rainbow of colors to white. This is called coral bleaching.

Fahrenheit
+0.5°
+1°
+1.5°
+2°
+2.5°
+3°

CANADA

UNITED STATES

MEXICO

Shielding Coral Reefs

The Great Barrier Reef off the coast of Australia is suffering from more and more bleaching, and organizations are working to protect it. Tiffany & Co. Foundation grants money to special projects. They are working with University of Melbourne to develop an ultra thin sun shield for coral reefs. It is 50,000 times thinner than human hair. It is designed to sit on top of the water over coral reefs during a heat wave. The film is **biodegradable** and can reduce, by up to 30 percent, the light exposure, that can cause bleaching.

Sometimes corals can recover from a bleaching event. However, if the water doesn't cool, they can starve to death.

9

OXYGEN FROM OCEANS

Oxygen in oceans comes from the photosynthesis **of marine plants. Water circulates the oxygen to deeper parts of the ocean. But as ocean waters warm, there are pockets of low or no oxygen.**

Warmer water holds less oxygen than cooler water. No marine life can survive without oxygen. Some low or no oxygen zones are found off the coast of California, Peru, Namibia, and the Arabian Sea. While some of these zones are natural, they are growing due to warmer waters.

Amount of oxygen in cool water vs warm water

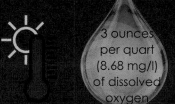

3.9 ounces per quart (10.92 mg/l) of dissolved oxygen

3 ounces per quart (8.68 mg/l) of dissolved oxygen

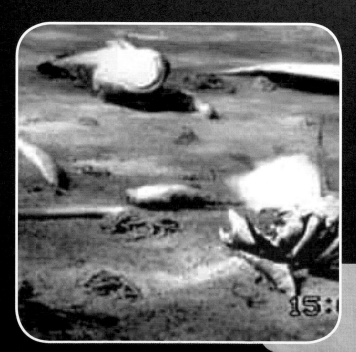

This underwater video frame shows crabs, fish, and clams killed by lack of oxygen on the sea floor in the western Baltic Sea.

Dylan Vecchione

Dylan is a 16-year-old diver who noticed coral reefs dying off the coast of Hawaii. He saw shrinking biodiversity and fading colors. He realized that most people haven't seen what's happening below sea level. So Dylan founded ReefQuest, a website where visitors can see the thousands of images of the reef Dylan has taken. He hopes it will encourage people to take action to save coral reefs.

Algae blooms look like thick mats covering the water's surface.

Algae Blooms

Another cause of low oxygen is algae blooms. Algae are small plants that float in the water. They multiply faster in warm water. They also thrive when fertilizers run off from land and increase **nutrients** in the water. When algae grow quickly, they create an algae bloom. It uses up all the oxygen in the water around it. We can reduce the growth of low-oxygen pockets in the oceans by decreasing the amount of fertilizer that we use on land so it doesn't wash into our oceans. Working to reduce greenhouse gases will help keep ocean temperatures cooler.

INCREASING ACIDITY

Climate change is making our ocean water more acidic. Acidic water is corrosive, which means it can eat away at solid materials. It threatens marine animals that have solid shells and skeletons, as well as some types of fish.

Acidic ocean water happens when the water absorbs too much carbon dioxide. For thousands of years, the amount of carbon dioxide (CO_2) in our air was **stable** and the acidity of the ocean never changed. But the more fossil fuels such as oil and gas that we use, the more carbon dioxide gets released into the air. The more CO_2 in the air, the more of it the ocean absorbs.

Where does our carbon dioxide go?

Stays in atmosphere
40%

Absorbed by oceans
30%

CO_2

Absorbed by trees and forests
30%

Emma Camp

Emma Camp is a biologist from Essex, England. She noticed that some types of coral have **adapted** to living in warmer, more acidic waters. She has the idea of transplanting some of these "super-survivor" corals onto reefs, such as the Great Barrier Reef, where corals are struggling. She reminds people, however, that the most important thing we can do to save coral reefs is to slow or reverse climate change.

Impact on Wildlife

Acidic ocean water makes it difficult for marine creatures to develop strong skeletons. It also does damage to hard outer shells and casings called exoskeletons. Oyster, clam, and lobster shells become thin and full of holes. Fish are sensitive to the acidity of the water around them. They use a lot of energy to keep their bodies in balance with it. This can result in stunted growth or a reduced ability to escape from predators or catch food. Studies have shown that ocean acidity can be decreased by planting more marine plants such as kelp, eelgrass, and seaweed, which take in CO_2. By keeping acidity low, it will give shellfish such as oysters a chance to grow hard, protective shells.

Damaged shells leave marine creatures with less protection from predators and the environment.

DANGEROUS WEATHER PATTERNS

Oceans near the equator absorb the heat created by the Sun's rays. Then, currents **move the warm water north and south, and bring cooler water back. This movement affects weather and climate around the world. As ocean temperatures rise, our weather patterns are changing.**

Flooding was a serious threat during Hurricane Sandy, which destroyed hundreds of thousands of homes and impacted millions of people.

Warmer oceans mean that stronger storms are forming. In the past 30 years, the number of tropical storms that have developed into powerful hurricanes has tripled. Increases in rainfall, wave height, and wind speed have been recorded in oceans across the globe. These changes can lead to more serious flooding and coastal **erosion**. Scientists say that Hurricane Sandy in 2012 would not have flooded Manhattan Island if it had happened 100 years earlier. That is because the sea was 1 foot (30 cm) lower at that time. Stormier seas also make shipping more dangerous and oil spills more likely.

Marinel Ubaldo

Marinel Ubaldo lost friends and family in Super Typhoon Haiyan, which hit Southeast Asia in 2013. She then decided to dedicate her life to fighting for climate justice. Ubaldo organized the Philippines' first youth climate strike in May 2019. She also testified in the Philippines for their Human Rights investigation into the role and responsibility of corporations in regards to climate change.

Tackling the Problem

Around the world, many scientists, organizations, and governments are working to reduce their use of fossil fuels to slow climate change. People are also trying to reduce the effects of extreme weather. Two researchers, Ryan Abernathey and Richard Seager, have developed a fleet of more than 3,000 **floats** that measure ocean temperature. By studying the data from these floats, they hope to predict extreme weather events and help communities better prepare for them.

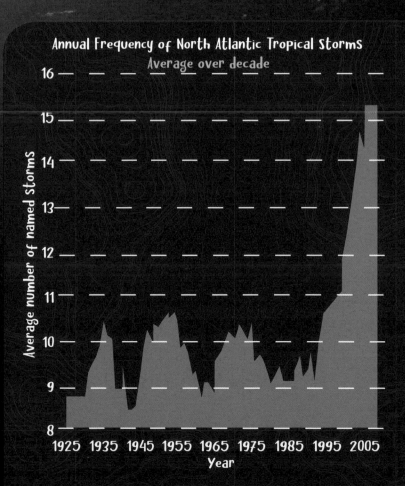

Annual Frequency of North Atlantic Tropical Storms
Average over decade

Average number of named storms

Year

CHANGING CURRENTS

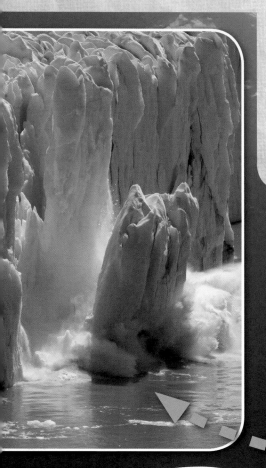

Climate change is affecting our oceans' currents. Scientists have found that the Atlantic Ocean's circulation has slowed about 15 percent since the middle of last century. This has led to seasonal changes, glacial **melting, and extreme weather.**

Slower currents have caused colder winters and hotter summers in Europe, changing rainfall in the tropics, more destructive storms, and warmer water building up along U.S. coasts causing sea level rise. Warmer temperatures mean glaciers are melting faster, and more icebergs are breaking off them and floating into shipping lanes.

10% of land area on Earth is covered with glacial ice. That's more than 5.8 million square miles (15 million square km).

Scientists are monitoring the changes in currents. The data they collect will help us understand what these changes will mean for weather patterns in the future.

Halting the Changes

Researchers believe the slower current is caused by the large amount of cold, fresh water from melting ice flowing into the ocean. Fresh water is not as dense as saltier ocean water. It does not sink down to help the movement of the water. Even more extreme weather will be created as the current slows. Scientists have noticed that this is also happening in the Antarctic currents. While these major currents are slowing, other smaller currents are speeding up due to faster and stronger winds.

Faster currents also change global weather patterns and damage marine **ecosystems.**

The best way to stop or slow these changes is to reduce climate change. By changing our habits, such as using less fossil fuel, we can reduce global greenhouse gases. Large companies can also work to release less carbon dioxide. Power plants are encouraged to use a carbon capture system and store their carbon dioxide instead of releasing it into the atmosphere.

SEA LEVEL SWELL

Scientists have noticed that the sea level is rising. Rising water threatens to overwhelm small island nations and coastal regions. It increases flooding, worsens hurricane damage, and leaches saltwater into tidal areas.

Eight of the world's largest coastal cities are threatened by flooding. Oceans have already risen by about 7.2 inches (18 cm) since the late 1800s. Since then, the rate of change has been speeding up. Some scientists say oceans could rise up to 6.5 feet (2 m) or more this century. The rise in sea level is caused by higher temperatures, which melt glaciers and ice packs. Water expands as it warms, which means a warmer ocean takes up more space than a colder ocean.

The coastal city of Venice has experienced extreme flooding.

OCEAN ACTION

Shalvi Sakshi

Shalvi Sakshi lives in Fiji and understands the threat of rising sea levels. The low-lying island nation could be completely underwater in the next few decades if sea levels continue to rise. Sakshi was the youngest speaker at the United Nations climate talks in 2017. She urged world leaders to stop the release of greenhouse gas **emissions** into the atmosphere.

Stopping the Rise

Researchers use tide stations and satellites to monitor sea levels. The only way to stop ice and glaciers from melting is to reduce the greenhouse gases that keep heat in our atmosphere. Solar power, wind power, and geothermal energy are ways to produce electricity, and to heat and cool our homes without increasing greenhouse gases. Vancouver, British Columbia, and Seattle, Washington, are two of 105 cities around the world with goals of reducing greenhouse gas emissions by at least 80% by the year 2050.

How long before cities are underwater?

1,000 years
65.6 ft (20 m)
New York

100 years
22.9 ft (7 m)
Shanghai

200 years
9.8 ft (3 m)
San Francisco

100 years
3.2 ft (1 m)
Venice

Many cities have installed defenses against flooding, such as these gates in London, England.

DIMINISHING COASTLINES

Around the world, about 200 million people live along coastlines. It allows them to be close to a food source, jobs, and transportation routes. But as sea levels rise, and extreme weather increases due to climate change, higher levels of coastal erosion are occurring.

Coastal erosion is the loss of land along coastlines due to rising sea levels, strong waves, and **storm surges**. The soil, rocks, and sand are carried away and deposited offshore. With climate change creating stronger winds and more violent storms, coastal erosion is increasing. The coast of Rhode Island is eroding faster due to waves and storm surges. The surges are going over natural sand dunes and flooding farther inland.

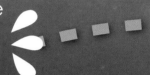

One of the world's fastest eroding coasts is the Holderness Coast in England. It is losing around 6.5 feet (2 m) per year.

OCEAN ACTION

Ridhima Pandey

Ridhima Pandey is a 12-year-old living in India. At age 9, she sued the Indian government in 2017 over its failure to address climate change. In her lawsuit, Pandey called on the government to reduce greenhouse gases, set aside money to work on projects, and create plans to deal with the effects of climate change. She joins other youth around the world such as Greta Thunberg of Sweden, who are demanding a global change to save our world.

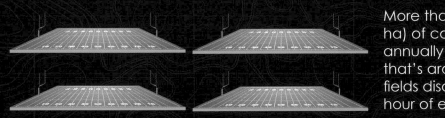

More than 80,000 acres (32,375 ha) of coastal wetlands are lost annually in the United States—that's around seven football fields disappearing every hour of every day.

1h

Protection From Erosion

Coastal communities are working to protect themselves from coastal erosion and storm surges. The Dutch city of Rotterdam has built a massive barrier that is the size of two Eiffel Towers on their sides. Volunteers on Prince Edward Island in Canada are helping to plant marram grass in sand dunes. The roots of this grass help to hold sand in place and act as a **buffer** against storm surges.

THREAT OF DISEASE

Changing ocean water means bacteria, viruses, and parasites **can thrive.** While cooler ocean water keeps these organisms in check, warm water allows them to live longer and spread farther. Changes in acidity and salt levels also affect these organisms. New diseases are spreading through the oceans and causing more damage to marine life.

Coral diseases have also increased with rising water temperatures.

Lobsters are facing a new threat because of warming oceans, called **epizootic** shell disease (ESD). Bacteria can invade a lobster's shell and kill it by making it difficult for the lobster to shed its shell to grow. Temperature is the main factor in the spread of this disease. It has caused the number of lobsters suffering from ESD to double in years that have a warmer spring or hotter summer waters.

In protected areas, coral reefs can recover up to 20% faster.

Saving Sea Stars

Sea stars in the Pacific are being devastated by a **wasting disease** caused by a virus that is more active in warmer conditions. Off California's coast, the sunflower sea star has been almost completely destroyed by sea star wasting disease (SSWD) since 2013. Sea stars keep purple sea urchin populations under control. Without the sea stars, the urchins eat ocean kelp forests right to the sea floor. Scientist Eric Littman, has developed a way to CT scan sea stars. It helps him see early signs of the disease. This will help him treat affected sea stars before it's too late. This can help restore sea star populations. Without slowing climate change, even more viral and bacterial diseases will continue to spread. One way to reduce greenhouse gases is to plant trees. Trees, including mangrove trees along coasts, take in CO_2 and make oxygen.

HABITATS AT RISK

As climate change alters the environment and habitats of marine plants and animals, they are struggling. Some species are leaving their habitats to find cooler water. Others try to adapt to warmer water.

As ocean temperatures rise, the types of species along coasts may change. The pelagic red crab washes onto California shores when Pacific waters are warm.

Stress and disease mean marine life is not growing as fast or reproducing as well. Some species are shifting their habitats to cooler water, which may expose them to higher acidity, salt levels, and new predators. Combined with people taking more and more seafood out of the ocean to eat, it means **fish stocks** are decreasing. Fewer fish and marine mammals in the ocean doesn't just affect the food supply for people—it also affects the food chain for other ocean dwellers. Around the world, fish stocks have dropped around 4 percent. Much of the current stocks are overfished or at **capacity**.

Red Snapper over time: average weight, age, size, and ability to reproduce

1962

21 lbs (9.5 kg)
11 years

33 inches (83.5 cm)

1985

7.2 lbs (3.3 kg)
4 years

23.5 inches
(60 cm)

TODAY

1 lb (0.5 kg)
2 years

16 inches
(40.6 cm)

= 100,000 eggs

Fishing regulations need to protect fish stocks.

Future in Question

A few species of fish are doing well in warmer water. Black sea bass numbers are up, but scientists warn that while they have responded well to the rise in temperature so far, they will likely begin to struggle if the rise continues. The best ways to protect fish stocks is to restore their environments to cooler, less acidic water. As well as reducing greenhouse gases to slow the heating up of our planet and our oceans, government fishing regulations need to change. In June 2019, Canada passed a new Fisheries Act. The new law requires Fisheries and Oceans Canada to manage fish stocks so they thrive, and to have a plan in place for species of marine creatures that are struggling.

GET INVOLVED

Slowing and reversing climate change will only happen if the world works together. We share our atmosphere and our oceans. All countries have to make changes that lower carbon dioxide and other greenhouse gas emissions.

World Oceans Day happens each year on June 8th. It is a good time to join in activities and programs to take action to protect our oceans. Beach cleanups, workshops, and photo exhibits are just some of the activities planned each year. The World Oceans Day Youth Advisory Council is a group of young people from around the world who get together to brainstorm ways to create change and keep oceans healthy.

OCEAN ACTION

UN Sustainable Development Goals

The United Nations (UN) is an organization that brings together almost 200 countries. Together, they create goals to improve life for everyone on our planet. Two of those goals are "Climate Action" and "Life Below Water." They are helping member nations to develop plans to tackle climate change, and to preserve and protect our oceans. For climate actions, countries agreed to keep greenhouse gas emissions down and use more renewable energy.

SUSTAINABLE DEVELOPMENT GOALS

The UN encourages youth to get involved and build a world they want to see in the future.

Stay Informed

It is also important to keep up to date with what is happening around the world. The Internet has current news and scientific studies. The latest scientific research is reported on sites such as Science Daily and Science News. There are several ocean websites that report on current numbers and data such as Ocean Conservancy and Deep Sea News.

YOU CAN MAKE A DIFFERENCE

We can also make changes on a personal level that can lessen climate change and the damage to our oceans. By reducing our fossil fuel and energy use in our daily lives, we can make a difference.

We use fossil fuels to run our cars, buses, airplanes, furnaces, and to generate electricity at some power plants. By choosing to walk or bike instead of taking a car, we are helping to decrease the carbon dioxide released into the air. Using less energy also helps control climate change because electricity is often generated using fossil fuels such as oil or natural gas. LED lightbulbs use far less energy than regular lightbulbs. Solar and wind power are renewable energy forms that will never run out. Solar and wind power also don't contribute to greenhouse gases. Adding solar panels to your roof to generate power helps reduce the amount you need from power plants.

Washing clothes in cold water and hanging them to dry instead of using a dryer can help save a lot of electricity.

Shopping local is one step we can take to help slow climate change. It means that trucks, ships, and planes did not bring the food to you.

FRESH LOCAL PRODUCE

Fighting for Change

We can also hold governments and businesses **accountable** for their roles in climate change and ocean pollution. One way is to write to local government representatives asking them to explain what efforts they are taking to slow climate change and protect our oceans. Another way is to support local businesses and restaurants that are doing their part in the fight against climate change. Some have already banned single-use plastics and increased their use of renewable energy. Protecting and preserving our oceans is everyone's responsibility.

GLOSSARY

accountable Having to explain your actions

acidic Containing acid; In oceans, carbon dioxide increases acidity.

adapted Made changes to thrive in new conditions

biodegradable Able to break down naturally

buffer Something that lessens the impact

capacity The maximum amount

coral cays Sandy islands formed on top of coral reefs

critical About to become a crisis

currents Water moving in a specific direction, usually through a larger body of water

ecosystems Communities of living things and their environments

emissions Things given off into the air

epizootic Temporarily widespread

erosion Wearing away of soil or rock

expel Force to leave

fish stocks Populations of fish

floats Devices that remain on the water's surface

glacial To do with glaciers, which are slow-moving masses of ice

leaches Seeps through or dissolves

migrate To move from one habitat to another

moderate Make less extreme

nutrients Substances that help living things grow and thrive

parasites Organisms that live on or in another organism and cause harm

photosynthesis Process plants use with sunlight to make food and oxygen from carbon dioxide and water

stable Staying at one level

storm surges Water pushed on shore by a storm's winds

wasting disease Disease that makes organisms thinner and weaker

LEARNING MORE

Books

Sjonger, Rebecca. *Taking Action to Help the Environment*. Crabtree Publishing Company, 2020.

Sneideman, Joshua, and Erin Twamley. *Climate Change: The Science Behind Melting Glaciers and Warming Oceans*. Nomad Press, 2020.

Thomas, Keltie. *Rising Seas: Flooding, Climate Change and Our New World*. Firefly Books, 2018.

Websites

https://bit.ly/2VI5r9Q
Travel with David Attenborough as he explores the Great Barrier Reef in this virtual tour.

https://climatekids.nasa.gov/ocean/
NASA's Climate Kids website dives into the question of what is happening in the ocean.

https://www.weather.gov/owlie/science_kt
The National Ocean Service (NOAA) website allows kids to explore weather science and storms.

INDEX

ABOUT THE AUTHOR

Natalie Hyde has written more than 90 fiction and non-fiction books for young readers. When she gets time to relax, one of her favorite places to be is beside the ocean on a warm, sandy beach.